DABO DAVIES

UNLOCKING SUPREME INTELLIGENCE

Understand how to operate and succeed with spiritual wisdom

Copyright © 2023, Dabo Davies

All rights reserved.
This book or any portion thereof may not be reproduced or used in any manner whatsoever without the express written permission of the publisher.

Printed in United Kingdom

ISBN: 9798852769602

DH Davies Global
London
United kingdom

WWW.DHDAVIES.ORG

DABO H. DAVIES

UNLOCKING SUPREME INTELLIGENCE

Understand how to operate and succeed with spiritual wisdom

Unlocking Supreme Intelligence

Acknowledgement

The bulk of the knowledge and intellect I possess to date, to the glory of God, derives first and foremost from a constant download of information and ideas by the Holy Spirit, as well as knowledge gleaned from various people who have powerfully impacted and taught me, directly and indirectly, along my life's journey thus far.

I am forever grateful to the countless exceptional people who, by their commitment and devotion to becoming the best they could be, have inspired me to do likewise.

I am forever grateful to my precious wife, Elizabeth, my wife of many years and mother to my lovely children, for her unmatched love, constant prayers, patience and support.

To my Household of Mercy family and the countless partners, who support us, exhibiting their love and passion, I say THANK YOU.

Contents

Acknowledgement v

Introduction 1

PART A:
THE NEED FOR SPIRITUAL INTELLIGENCE 13

Chapter 1: Love and Betrayal 15

Chapter 2: The Inteligent Tribe... 27

Chapter 3: When You Leverage on Supreme
Intelligence 43

Chapter 4: The Kiss and The Sword 67

PART B:
HOW TO GATHER SPIRITUAL
INTELLIGENCE... 83

Chapter 5: Learning The Art of Spiritual
Mapping 85

Chapter 6: How to Secure the Anointing for *Discernment* 97

Chapter 7: How to Respond to Divine Intelligence 103

Introduction

"You'll remember, friends, that when I first came to you to let you in on God's sheer genius, I didn't try to impress you with polished speeches and the latest philosophy. I deliberately kept it plain and simple: first Jesus and who He is; then Jesus and what He did—Jesus crucified.

I was unsure of how to go about this, and felt totally inadequate—I was scared to death, if you want the truth of it—and so nothing I said could have impressed you or anyone else. But the Message came through anyway. God's Spirit and God's power did it, which made it clear that your life of faith is a response to God's power, not to some fancy mental or emotional footwork by me or anyone else.

We, of course, have plenty of wisdom to pass on to you once you get your feet on firm spiritual ground, but ***it's not popular wisdom***, the fashionable wisdom of high-priced experts that will be out-of-date in a year or so. ***God's wisdom is something mysterious that goes deep into the interior of his purposes.*** You don't find it lying around on the surface. It's not the latest message, but more like the oldest—what God determined as the way to bring out his best in us, long before we ever arrived on the scene. The experts of our day haven't a clue about what this eternal plan is. If they had, they wouldn't have killed the Master of the God-designed life on a cross. That's why we have this Scripture text:

No one's ever seen or heard anything like this,
Never so much as imagined anything quite like it—
What God has arranged for those who love him.

But *you've* seen and heard it because God by his Spirit has brought it all out into the open before you.

10-13 The Spirit, not content to flit around on the surface, dives into the depths of God, and brings out what God planned all along. Whoever knows what you're thinking and planning except you yourself? The same with God—except that he not only knows what he's thinking, but he lets *us* in on it. God

Introduction

offers a full report on the gifts of life and salvation that he is giving us. We don't have to rely on the world's guesses and opinions. We didn't learn this by reading books or going to school; we learned it from God, who taught us person-to-person through Jesus, and we're passing it on to you in the same first-hand, personal way.

¹⁴⁻¹⁶ The unspiritual self, just as it is by nature, can't receive the gifts of God's Spirit. There's no capacity for them. They seem like so much silliness. Spirit can be known only by spirit—God's Spirit and our spirits in open communion. Spiritually alive, we have access to everything God's Spirit is doing, and can't be judged by unspiritual critics. Isaiah's question, "Is there anyone around who knows God's Spirit, anyone who knows what he is doing?" has been answered: Christ knows, and we have Christ's Spirit."

- 1 Corinthians 2:1-16 - The Message Translation

¹⁸⁻²¹ The Message that points to Christ on the Cross seems like sheer silliness to those hellbent on destruction, but for those on the way of salvation it makes perfect sense. This is the

way God works, and most powerfully as it turns out. It's written,

I'll turn conventional wisdom on its head,
I'll expose so-called experts as shams.

So where can you find someone truly wise, truly educated, truly intelligent in this day and age? Hasn't God exposed it all as pretentious nonsense? Since the world in all its fancy wisdom never had a clue when it came to knowing God, God in his wisdom took delight in using what the world considered stupid—*preaching*, of all things!—to bring those who trust him into the way of salvation.

22-25 While Jews clamor for miraculous demonstrations and Greeks go in for philosophical wisdom, we go right on proclaiming Christ, the Crucified. Jews treat this like an *anti*-miracle—and Greeks pass it off as absurd. But to us who are personally called by God himself—both Jews and Greeks—Christ is God's ultimate miracle and wisdom all wrapped up in one. Human wisdom is so cheap, so impotent, next to the seeming absurdity of God. Human strength can't begin to compete with God's "weakness."

26-31 Take a good look, friends, at who you were when you got called into this life. I don't see many of "the brightest and the

Introduction

best" among you, not many influential, not many from high-society families. Isn't it obvious that God deliberately chose men and women that the culture overlooks and exploits and abuses, chose these "nobodies" to expose the hollow pretensions of the "somebodies"? That makes it quite clear that none of you can get by with blowing your own horn before God. Everything that we have—right thinking and right living, a clean slate and a fresh start—comes from God by way of Jesus Christ. That's why we have the saying, "If you're going to blow a horn, blow a trumpet for God."

- 1 Corinthians 1:18-31 - The Message Translation

[13] Who among you is wise and intelligent? Let him by his good conduct show his [good] deeds with the gentleness and humility of true wisdom. [14] But if you have bitter jealousy and selfish ambition in your hearts, do not be arrogant, and [as a result] be in defiance of the truth. [15] This [superficial] wisdom is not that which comes down from above, but is earthly (secular), natural (unspiritual), even demonic. [16] For where jealousy and selfish ambition exist, there is disorder [unrest,

> rebellion] and every evil thing and morally degrading practice. ⁱ⁷ But the wisdom from above is first pure [morally and spiritually undefiled], then peace-loving [courteous, considerate], gentle, reasonable [and willing to listen], full of compassion and good fruits. It is unwavering, without [self-righteous] hypocrisy [and self-serving guile]. ¹⁸ And the seed whose fruit is righteousness (spiritual maturity) is sown in peace by those who make peace [by actively encouraging goodwill between individuals].
>
> **- James 3:13-18 - Amplified Bible**

Have you ever eaten and savoured the taste of a delicious meal or admired with awe the wonder of a gigantic artistic masterpiece?

How do you feel when you hear the beautiful sound of a well-composed musical symphony or feel the love of a doting mother, watch with glued passion, her dutiful husband? And how does it feel when you enjoy the compassion of friendship?

Introduction

Every meaningful action is an intelligent art...

It is interesting to appreciate that there is art in various aspects of life all around us. The creativity expressed through art has made a significant contribution to every sphere of human activity.

When art is devoid of a considerable measure of intelligence and creativity, it loses its harmony, beauty and worth. The appreciation and performance of intelligent art are based on how we employ and exercise our physical senses.

The reality is, physical actions and events are consistently sending signals and sensations to the natural senses for assessment and appreciation.

Picture in your imagination, an energetic dance in the dark, or the sound of a beautiful song. The human senses give life and meaning to every activity, without which a man or woman may be disconnected from his or her environment.

In the physical realm, there are several kinds of abilities and intelligence, which range from emotional, artificial, analytical, mental and relational intelligence, to mention just a few. These kinds of intelligence often provide more refined and highly valuable abilities, relationships, goods, services, and experiences in the temporal realm.

However, natural senses are significantly limited and inadequate in providing for the greatest needs of man, which are: a sense of purpose, genuine fulfilment and advantage in the realm above the natural.

Do you believe that there is a spiritual realm?

The truth is, the tangible emerged from the intangible; the visible appeared from the invisible, and the physical is a manifestation of the spiritual. The outcome of purposes, actions, activities and events in the spirit realm are manifest in our physical experiences.

There is a lot to learn about what's going on around you! Therefore, you cannot continually live in oblivion to the realities that lie in the realm of the Spirit. You have to learn to become familiar with the unfamiliar, walk on water like dry land; see the invisible, and believe the unbelievable if you desire to achieve the impossible.

You need spiritual intelligence.

Unlocking Spiritual Intelligence is about man's ability to utilize his spiritual senses to discern intentions, activities, signals and sensations that are often veiled in the physical realm.

In the language of technology today, look at it as divine intel.

These sensations will form the basis of your perspectives, decisions, direction, stability and sustenance in life.

Therefore, we ought not to limit ourselves to only what we can see.

There has to be more to what we see. You have to recognize and exercise your divine intelligence like the children of Issachar.

I believe that our ability to access divine intelligence and operate with depends on these two things:

1. Our relationship with God

2. Our effective communication with God. Emphasis is on 'effective', because we must go beyond talking and be willing to listen to what God has to say.

A lack of divine intelligence affects our operational method and causes us to function outside the specific pattern God has prescribed for each one of us.

This book was birthed on request by people whose lives were impacted by our virtual prayer sessions. It has been carefully written to provide you with insight into how you can recognize and exercise your spiritual senses for a more complete and prosperous life.

Congratulations! You are holding in your hands a book that has the potential to activate and sharpen your discernment and empower you with the ability to function beyond the limited realm of the physical.

Therefore, don't just think about acting - *Act Now*!

In an era where foolishness is accepted and believed when cloaked in eloquence and charisma, the need for spiritual/divine intelligence cannot be over emphasised.

Introduction

Regardless of what people think, the reality is, positive results are achieved by taking action, rather than just mere words.

There is a difference between people who excel and those who don't, between those who win and those who don't; *"WINNERS see, speak and ACT while LOSERS look, talk and slack".*

The point here is, your words must be commensurate with your faith and action.

Frankly, no matter how powerful the teachings, instructions and prayer points are in this book, it will not benefit you in anyway if it makes an interesting read only, without one following the steps to action.

You might just as well stop reading now if you are NOT going to do anything. But hey! I do believe you can make it through to massive action from the lessons you acquire here.

So, get ready to act, pray and manifest.

Unlocking Supreme Intelligence

PART A
The Need for Spiritual Intelligence

Unlocking Supreme Intelligence

CHAPTER 1
Love and Betrayal

"Stab the body and it heals but, injure the heart and the wound lasts a lifetime."
— *Mineko Iwasak*

Love and trust are sacred gifts...

A wise man once said, "When hope is crushed, the heart is crushed, but a wish come true fills you with joy". Love and trust always come with their demands and expectations.

Moreover, it is evident that the fuel of every human relationship in business and family is the sacred gift of love and trust.

Love is so amazing and beautiful even in the face of hate and adversity; it triumphs. Also, trust is relieving and peaceful when it is shared with someone who has earned it through consistent loyalty.

There are, however, times when we love someone more than they love us or trust people who haven't been steadily true to us. It is no strange feeling to get so upset about how stupid, crazy or foolish it seems when we offer our pearl to swine.

Well, just before you lose heart; you need to realize that this can be one of the bravest things you can do in life.

However, there is a place for discernment when you are in a love and trust relationship with anyone.

> *"For there to be betrayal, there would have to have been trust first."*
> **— Suzanne Collins, The Hunger Games**

Love can seem unfair...

How does it feel when you truly love someone without condition or expectation of reciprocation? How about loving people who seem imperfect and flawed?

Do you know that you can still cherish, serve, and forgive the same people who have broken their promises, said unintentionally hurtful things, fallen short or forgotten something special to you?

The truth is, sometimes love makes us vulnerable.

A better understanding of the dynamics of love and the evaluation of its reliability is provided by emotional, interpersonal and mental intelligence.

But the truth is these forms of intelligence are significantly limited. Natural intelligence judges people and relationships by the signs, signals, indicators, occurrences and happenings at the physical and mental levels.

Spiritual/divine intelligence surpasses natural intelligence because it goes further and pierces into the intangible and unreachable aspects of our experiences, choices, perceptions and observations.

Its' depth uncovers inner motives and thoughts that cannot be discerned in the physical.

Though we are encouraged to love unconditionally and trust wholeheartedly, there is a place for knowledge, discernment and spiritual intelligence.

There is protection, direction, fulfilment and greater advantage in leveraging on spiritual discernment. Personally, I have discovered that one of the easiest ways the enemy can gain access to us, infiltrate our camps and frustrate our efforts, is through love relationships or partnerships based on trust.

This is because people tend to become vulnerable when in love.

This is the kind of vulnerability that exists because, in love, we are motivated to trust the other person with so much based on little or nothing more than just affectionate feelings and emotional attachment.

Consequently, we let our guards down, sleep with two eyes closed, douse suspicion and impede logical judgement when we are wrapped up in love and affection towards anyone.

You may have lived out these facts in your personal lives, where you trusted fully, gave unquestioned loyalty, threw carefulness, caution and doubt to the wind and loved wholeheartedly, only to be thoroughly betrayed.

Now, you find that you have begun to put a check upon your minds and perhaps, question your desires and ability to be that vulnerable, to love again.

It is understood that betrayal is a scary possibility and can become a major impediment in every love and trust relationship.

On many occasions, even as we have read about in the Bible, for instance as told of Judas and Jesus, Samson and Delilah, the perpetrators were those in a close relationship, who initially had no intention to betray, but became engulfed by weakness, greed, pressure; words were spoken, things were misconceived or misconstrued.

If you investigate carefully, you will discover that the people that betray, especially those who were very close to you, may not have entertained any intention to betray you, but access was granted, words were spoken, things were misconceived or misconstrued, and sometimes promises were made and a full betrayal happened.

Lessons from the Valley of Sorek

The book of Judges chapter 16 throws light on this fact with the story of Samson and Delilah

> *"Later on, he [Samson] fell in love with a girl named Delilah over in the valley of Sorek. The five heads of the Philistine nation went personally to her and demanded that she find out from Samson what made him so strong, so that they would know how to overpower and subdue him and put him in chains.*
>
> *"Each of us will give you a thousand dollars for this job," they promised."*
> **— Judges 16:4-6 – The Living Bible**

Love and Betrayal

We have looked at this story from the angle of love displayed by Samson, but it is also important to point out that Samson's seduction, manipulation and betrayal happened because of intrusion from external forces.

Subtly and heinously, the heads of the Philistine nation went personally to Delilah, demanding that she seduce the man who loved her and probably whom she also loved.

Delilah bought into the demands of Samson's enemies for the sake of the huge reward. She quickly knew what to do, to force out the mystery behind Samson's god-like strength. She perfected her plans, sharpened her tongue and Samson was naive and in love; this made him a perfect prey.

So, it is time to silence the voice of treachery.

You may not realise it, but people are speaking into the ears of the people you love, the people you are connected to, the people you are in sync with, and the people that are supposed to support your vision. Conspirators are speaking into the ears and minds of your business partners and the people that are strategically positioned to favour you on your job.

Guard your contacts against infiltration.

We must be very sensitive to guard the relationships we have, mostly in prayer because the enemy will constantly attempt to gain access to us through the people very close to us.

One of the strategies deployed by the enemy in systematically dismantling what you are building is through *infiltration.*

The dictionary defines INFILTRATION as;

> *"the action of entering or gaining access to an organization or place surreptitiously, especially to acquire secret information or cause damage."*

We must be discerning because not everyone attempting to access your lives, vision, families, ideas, etc. has a clear motive to support or build with you. Some are deployed by the enemy to gain access to valuable and strategic information that can delay, dismantle and completely destroy what you have been allocated.

Love and Betrayal

Just like a magnet attracts all types of metals irrespective of their usefulness. Your anointing attracts all types of people, some with good intentions and some not. It is however, your responsibility to intentionally identify the usefulness of everyone attracted to your anointing, idea, vision, or influence.

Everyone trying to build sustainably must build objectively, no matter the project.

We should love people, care for them and learn to show kindness, but decisions that relate to our vision or lives should not be taken sentimentally.

Every question either internally or externally that relates to the source of our power, the uniqueness of our idea, or the distinct nature of our systems and structures must be answered objectively with a certain measure of caution.

This was a mistake made by Samson. For the fact that Delilah had asked him severally the source of his power and made attempts to sabotage him should have been a clear indication that something was wrong.

Love should not blind your objectivity.

When your heart is in love, please don't switch off your mind.

Prayer against the Voice of Betrayal:

1. I declare that God will expose and expel every voice speaking betrayal and discord in the ears of the people I love, the people I am aligned to. I declare that the fire of God will be released and make every spirit of betrayal uncomfortable, uncovered and utterly destroyed, in Jesus' name.

2. I declare that everyone in the place of leadership just like the heads of the Philistine nation making attempts to sabotage my relationships, scheming and scamming, making promises with an intention to frustrate my efforts, hinder and limit my productivity, that they would be exposed and expelled in Jesus' name.

3. I declare that my relationships are secured, and the people I love are secured in the name of Jesus.

Love and Betrayal

4. I declare that God will frustrate the efforts of anyone or group of people attempting to sabotage my strategic relationships in all spheres of influence.

5. I pray for the people around me, those whose destinies are intertwined with mine, that their decisions are not made from deception. But rather, that they have access to divine information, and their decisions are free from prejudice and hypocrisy.

6. I pray for everyone connected to me that they will not fall victim to any satanic plot because of their vulnerabilities.

7. I declare that everyone connected to me possesses the ability and strength of character to withstand the alluring of the enemy with the intention to take advantage of them

8. I prayerfully build a spiritual firewall around everyone connected to me with vital information regarding my assignment, family, and business. I

declare that they are protected from demonic onslaught and manipulation.

9. I declare that everyone around me has the spiritual security system and sensitivity to monitor, and control foil every incoming attack based on the premise of God's word.

10. I declare that the people around me can discern both trusted and untrusted hands of fellowship, in Jesus name, Amen.

CHAPTER 2
The Inteligent Tribe

> *"To these four young men God gave knowledge and understanding of all kinds of literature and learning. And Daniel could understand visions and dreams of all kinds."*
> — ***Daniel 1:17 – New International Version***

We live in a day and age where discernment is a greatly needed gift in the body of Christ but also in every sphere of society.

It is important to remind ourselves that we are without doubt in a season of many divine shifts, and every leader and every believer needs the influence, that divine and special intelligence that was upon the Children of Issachar, in order not to miss out on what God is doing in this generation.

This influence will help you perceive the divine agenda and unmask every of the enemy's hidden plans.

This Chapter will inform and give you an understanding of this intelligent tribe, these unique individuals whose insight, skill and discerning ability amplified their relevance in an entire nation. You will be challenged and motivated to desire a kind of intelligence, knowledge and wisdom that comes divinely, that kind that is described in James chapter 3, the wisdom from above.

> "13 Who is wise and understanding among you? By his good conduct let him show his works in the meekness of wisdom. 14 But if you have bitter jealousy and selfish ambition in your hearts, do not boast and be false to the truth. 15 This is not the wisdom that comes down from above, but is earthly, unspiritual, demonic. 16 For where jealousy and selfish ambition exist, there will be disorder and every vile practice. 17 But the wisdom from above is first pure, then peaceable,

> gentle, open to reason, full of mercy and good fruits, impartial and sincere. ¹⁸ And a harvest of righteousness is sown in peace by those who make peace."
>
> **- James 3:13-18 – English Standard Version**

I want to bring to your attention once again that, in this generation, God is raising strategic men and women who will stand in influential capacities, endowed with abilities to manifest the purpose of God in dimensions after the order of the children of Issachar.

This book will help you attain greater knowledge, deeper insight, sharper discernment and a broader understanding of times, seasons, events, choices and situations in your life, career, business and ministry.

First, who was Issachar?

To understand the background of the Children of Issachar, you need to know who their father was. According to the book of Genesis 30:18, Issachar was Jacob's ninth son among twelve. His Mother was Leah, Jacob's first wife.

Interestingly, the name Issachar emphasises a reward. It also implies someone who will bring in reward upon investment.

Furthermore, when Jacob blessed all his sons, his prophetic description of Issachar was:

> "*Issachar is a STRONG DONKEY, crouching between the sheepfolds.*"
> — ***Gen 49:14 – English Standard Version***

The symbolism and meanings associated with donkeys give us an insight into the attributes and characteristics of the sons of Issachar.

In many cultures, donkeys are seen as a symbol of strength and courage. They are also often used as a symbol of wisdom and knowledge.

The versatility of the donkey is worth paying attention to.

As a symbol **of strength and determination**, the donkey is often used to represent someone who works hard and never gives up. As a symbol of humility and simplicity, the donkey reminds us that we don't need material possessions or power to be happy.

The donkey as a symbol of stubbornness is not necessarily a bad thing in this context because it emphasizes its tenacity and perseverance.

Donkeys are considered intelligent and possess a robust work ethic.

They are also reliable, practical, and down-to-earth. Donkeys are agile and have a good sense of balance, which makes them excellent climbers. The combination of their strength and gentle nature is commendable.

Beyond the physical characteristics of the donkey, it is considered to be dependable in challenging situations.

These attributes of the donkey are illustrative of the children of Issachar. They are smart, reliable and safety conscious. They have the ability to stop, study and sensibly assess the matter through, when faced with a challenging or frightening situation, unlike a horse which makes them a good partner on the trail.

Worthy of note again, is that Issachar became a tribe among the nation of Israel that was renowned for supreme and spiritual intelligence with which the nation was moved from obscurity into limelight.

Hence, it suffices to say that Issachar was a symbol of supreme knowledge, discernment and Spiritual intelligence. Therefore, you can easily deduce why, no investment on Issachar could have been wasted.

So, who were the Children of Issachar?

Our focus is on this outstanding group of people in Israel who emerged from the Tribe of Issachar. They were men of great skill above any of their neighbours.

The children of Issachar had a sound understanding of the times and seasons with which they charted the course of their nation on political, religious and business matters.

Indeed, the children of Issachar could be regarded as extraordinary individuals. The nation of Israel regarded the excellence of the descendants of Issachar in matters that relate to spiritual and natural strategy for advancement in business, public affairs and worship.

The children of Issachar brought tremendous rewards to everyone who recognized their influence and gleaned from their wisdom.

Armed with Knowledge and Discernment

> *"And of the children of Issachar, which were men that had understanding of the times, to **KNOW** what Israel ought to do; the heads of them were two hundred; and all their brethren were at their commandment."*
> *— 1 Chronicles 12:32 KJV*

The word **'Know'** in

1 Chronicles 12:32 is the Hebrew word **'Yada'**, which is the same word as **'Discern'**. Furthermore, it means *'to know'*, in reality, *to ascertain by seeing*.

The word- **"Ascertain"**, means to find out definitely, learn with certainty, and rest in assurance of the true identity and character of what has been discovered.

By implication, this indicates that the children of Issachar were not guessers. They never did anything by assumption or presumption, and they were not the **'maybe' or 'Yes and No'** children.

The children of Issachar were never indecisive. There were no instances where they were caught up in the valley of decision, not knowing what to do. These people were never double minded.

They were people who demonstrated clarity and confidence on every level.

The Children of Issachar were people who spoke with certainty, not by their intellectual prowess nor analytical abilities alone, but by the influence and insight of the Holy Spirit who has access to everything, everywhere and everyone.

> [11] For what person perceives (knows and understands) what passes through a man's thoughts except the man's own spirit within him? Just so no one discerns (comes to know and comprehend) the thoughts of God except the Spirit of God.
>
> [12] Now we have not received the spirit [that belongs to] the world, but the [Holy] Spirit Who is from God, [given to us] that we might realize and comprehend and appreciate the gifts [of divine favor and blessing so freely and lavishly] bestowed on us by God.
>
> [13] And we are setting these truths forth in words not taught by human wisdom but taught by the [Holy] Spirit, combining and interpreting spiritual truths with spiritual language [to those who possess the Holy Spirit].
>
> **- 1 Corinthians 2:11-13 – Amplified Bible, Classic Edition**

The sons of Issachar were so sharp and spiritually astute that the whole nation depended on them to know what they ought to do and when they ought to do it.

These people did not just know what to do, they also had a good understanding of timing.

This concept of timing is important because doing the right thing at the wrong time can attract an undesired result.

Applying a skill without the consideration of the right timing can come across as incompetence.

The importance of timing.

The book of Ecclesiastes 3:1, The Amplified Bible, Classic Edition reads;

"To everything, there is a season and a time for every matter or purpose under heaven"

Timing is a valuable resource, but without understanding the value of this resource, you won't have the motivation to prioritize it in your life.

We have seen several examples in the bible that illustrate the significance of time, like when Abraham got up 'early

The Inteligent Tribe

in the morning' while complying with God's instruction to sacrifice his only son (Genesis 22:1-3).

The phrase 'early in the morning' is illustrative that there was no form of hesitation in him. It was clear that Abraham understood the instruction and therefore, did not hesitate in obeying, and I would add, very quickly too.

Additionally, the sons of Issachar also excelled in the knowledge of God's law. They were full of wisdom.

Whenever Israel went into a battle or moved their camp, God instructed them to move in a specific order behind the cloud so that Judah, Issachar, and Zebulun always moved ahead of the tabernacle.

Because of their astounding qualities, the sons of Issachar became one of the tribes in movement formation for Israel as instructed by God.

The divine arrangement was, Judah (the praising people) went first; then Issachar (the wise and discerning ones) and Zebulun (the financiers). That's quite a combination!

> "¹⁴ The divisions of the camp of Judah went first, under their standard. Nahshon son of Amminadab was in command. ¹⁵ Nethanel son of Zuar was over the division of the tribe of Issachar, ¹⁶ and Eliab son of Helon was over the division of the tribe of Zebulun."
>
> **- Numbers 10:14-16 – New International Version**

The above verses in Numbers 10 highlight the significance of the involvement of the children of Issachar in leadership in the nation of Israel.

HERE ARE 2 SUPERB INSTANCES THAT HIGHLIGHT THE RELEVANCE OF THE CHILDREN OF ISSACHAR IN ISRAEL

A. THEY WENT AGAINST THE POPULAR OPINION

One remarkable thing about the Children of Issachar was the fact that they were not carried away by the majority vote. They were people of strong convictions on matters within the nation because of their discerning ability.

How did they demonstrate this?

You can find the answer in Judges Chapter 5. Here, it was recorded that, the Children of Issachar pledged their support to a female ruler. What a laudable stance!

This happened during the period when Israel was governed by judges, before it had Kings (around 1100 BC or earlier according to some scholars), a woman rose to Judge the land. Her name was Deborah.

Although women did have rights in Israel, it would still have been unusual for a woman to sit in authority over the nation. Yet, this exceptional tribe were able to recognize Deborah's influence, inner strength and wisdom that qualified her to be a matchless female Judge in Israel.

Also, this time was a tempestuous time for Israel. She was invaded by Amalekites who subdued the nation and reduced them to sticks and stones. Nevertheless, God was with Deborah. He placed her in authority, and the sons of Issachar knew it.

Therefore, they sided with Deborah and went out to battle under her leadership. Consequently, they gained a great victory and freed the land from foreign rule as a result.

Unlocking Supreme Intelligence

This suggests to us that having access to supreme intelligence can give you the courage to defy popular opinion and commit yourself to a person, organisation or vision that otherwise, would appear insignificant.

The tribe of Issachar backed the leadership of Deborah when other tribes were reluctant to support.

> "¹⁵The princes of Issachar were with Deborah; yes, Issachar was with Barak, sent under his command into the valley. In the districts of Reuben there was much searching of heart.
> ¹⁶ Why did you stay among the sheep pens to hear the whistling for the flocks?
> In the districts of Reuben there was much searching of heart.
> ¹⁷ Gilead stayed beyond the Jordan. And Dan, why did he linger by the ships?
> Asher remained on the coast
> and stayed in his coves."
>
> **- Judges 5:15-17 – New International Version**

B. THEY UNDERSTOOD DIVINE SELECTION AND APPOINTMENT.

The second instance when the Children of Issachar demonstrated supreme intelligence was when they supported King David before he became king; a period when Saul was still in power.

Before King David began to reign, warriors from the twelve (12) tribes started gathering to him, and the tribe of Issachar were part of that group.

Why did all of Issachar support David?

The tribe of Issachar supported David because they knew that God had called him to become king. Likewise, they knew the time was right to crown him King over God's people - Israel.

They could discern the changing of the times.

The significance of this show of support from the tribe of Issachar tribe and other tribes in fighting alongside David until he became king is worth mentioning, considering in our world today, the majority could be blinded politically because of projections from opinion polls, following and endorsing leaders who have not been selected nor instituted by God.

It becomes a rare occurrence to find a group of people endorse and follow an individual, a political party, or even an idea that does not have any physical indication of validation from God, but yet they are chosen and appointed by God.

The question is, can you risk being ostracised, rejected and ignored by influential people around you and the majority to support an individual or organisation just because you have divine insight about their vision or mandate?

Can you support an idea that is against the crowd?

The good news is we can all function with the same level of spiritual intelligence like the sons of Issachar.

We can have the influence, anointing and abilities the sons of Issachar possessed.

We can have the same power to discern the times and seasons in order to move in the right direction for our lives!

Praise God!

CHAPTER 3
When You Leverage on Supreme Intelligence

> ² "See, I have called by name Bezalel, son of Uri, the son of Hur, of the tribe of Judah. ³ I have filled him with the Spirit of God in wisdom and skill, in understanding and intelligence, in knowledge, and in all kinds of craftsmanship, ⁴ to make artistic designs for work in gold, in silver, and in bronze, ⁵ and in the cutting of stones for settings, and in the carving of wood, to work in all kinds of craftsmanship."
>
> **- Exodus 31:2-5 – Amplified Bible**

In this chapter we will examine the impact of supreme intelligence on businesses and spiritual progress of other individuals who leveraged on this higher power.

First, this chapter will help you realize that supreme intelligence and spiritual discernment is not an influence reserved for a tribe in medieval or modern Israel. You, too, can walk in divine abilities anywhere, any time and regardless of who you are.

God remains the same yesterday, today and forever. What He did for men of old, He can do for you and I today, Amen.

You will discover the devastating effect of walking in what the bible describes as the wisdom of this world without appropriate acknowledgement of the wisdom and direction that comes from God. This awareness will warn you about walking solely in your own understanding. Instead, in all your ways, you will increasingly acknowledge the power of God for progress, protection, prosperity and fulfilment.

> [18] "Let no person deceive himself. If anyone among you supposes that he is wise in this age, let him become a fool [let him discard his worldly discernment and recognize himself as dull, stupid, and foolish, without true learning and scholarship], that he may become [really] wise.
>
> [19] For this world's wisdom is foolishness (absurdity and stupidity) with God, for it is written, He lays hold of the wise in their [own] craftiness;"
>
> **- 1 Corinthians 3:18-19 – Amplified Bible, Classic Edition**

So, let's get started!

WHEN YOU LEVERAGE ON SUPREME INTELLIGENCE TO RUN A BUSINESS AND BUILD A CAREER

In Ecclesiastes 3:1, we read that there is a time for everything and a season for every activity under the heavens.

Research shows that the success of any venture hinges on wise choices and informed decisions.

For businesses, organizations, men and women who drive commerce and inventions, scientific reports or news headlines, business leads and expert recommendations are crucial to help chart the course of success; however, these expert projections and analyses are limited significantly.

Consequently, there is an emphasis on discernment, knowledge and intelligence above the natural realm. We all need divine guidance to navigate through the intricacies of life.

Abraham versus Lot

By divine guidance, Abraham settled in a more significant land in terms of size, and became very prosperous, even though he allowed Lot to make the first pick.

God showed him the limitless possibilities that awaited, and God is willing and able to reveal to you and me, when we rely on supreme intelligence.

Let's give some background to this story.

Abram and his nephew, Lot, both prospered while living in the land of Canaan. Their servants began to argue over whose flocks and herds should have the available grass. To solve the problem, Abram told Lot to choose an area for himself and that he (Abram) would take what was left. Lot chose the part of the land that appeared more fertile based on logical and physical assessment, moved over and settled there. Abram began living in a portion of land that physically was less fertile, but God blessed him and told him that all of that land would someday belong to his descendants.

Genesis 13:8-18 – New International Version

[8] "So Abram said to Lot, "Let's not have any quarrelling between you and me, or between your herders and mine, for we are close relatives.

[9] Is not the whole land before you? Let's part company. If you go to the left, I'll go to the right; if you go to the right, I'll go to the left."

[10] Lot looked around and saw that the whole plain of the Jordan toward Zoar was well watered, like the garden of the Lord, like the land of Egypt. (This was before the Lord destroyed Sodom and Gomorrah.)

[11] So Lot chose for himself the whole plain of the Jordan and

> set out toward the east. The two men parted company:
> ¹² Abram lived in the land of Canaan, while Lot lived among the cities of the plain and pitched his tents near Sodom.
> ¹³ Now the people of Sodom were wicked and were sinning greatly against the Lord.
> ¹⁴ The Lord said to Abram after Lot had parted from him, "Look around from where you are, to the north and south, to the east and west.
> ¹⁵ All the land that you see I will give to you and your offspring forever.
> ¹⁶ I will make your offspring like the dust of the earth, so that if anyone could count the dust, then your offspring could be counted.
> ¹⁷ Go, walk through the length and breadth of the land, for I am giving it to you."
> ¹⁸ So Abram went to live near the great trees of Mamre at Hebron, where he pitched his tents. There he built an altar to the Lord."

The Bible verses above highlight the consequences of working with intelligence influenced by your natural eyes and understanding.

For particular emphasis, verse 10 of Genesis 13 highlights the deception that our senses bring. It says Lot looked around and saw that the whole plain of the Jordan toward Zoar was well watered, like the garden of the Lord, like the land of Egypt.

Lot trusted his senses, while Abraham looked at the Lord, trusting divine intelligence.

Unknown to Lot, he had settled on a land where the people were wicked and were sinning greatly against the Lord.

There is always a limitation placed on decisions and choices made with the influence of the natural senses.

Lot saw the green pastures of the plain of the Jordan toward Zoar, and without careful deliberation, he pitched his tent towards the east.

He chose what appealed to his senses.

If we read further down into Genesis 14, Lot encountered problems on the seemingly green pastured land he chose and was taken captive, but then was rescued by Abram.

Lot was a victim of the limitations imposed by natural intelligence. He was devoid of divine perception and spiritual intelligence.

So, here's the difference?

An individual who operates with supreme intelligence does not necessarily have to choose first, go first, or even speak first.

Just like Abram, their connection with God allows them access to a superior knowledge and a deeper understanding that provides confidence in God's plans and agenda for their life and location.

A lack of discernment glued Lot's affection to the beautiful opportunities in front of him while he remained blinded from the looming disasters ahead.

Abram's prosperity did not surprise him because he acted in line with divine intelligence that always delivers incredible results.

Consider how valuable it will be to have divine intelligence enabling you to make investment decisions, knowing when and where to invest, what to invest in, and how to invest.

Imagine what hat great results would come forth.

WHEN YOU LEVERAGE ON DISCERNMENT FOR WORSHIP, MINISTRY AND SPIRITUAL PROGRESS

Another admirable ability of the children of Issachar was their knowledge of ceremonial or worship times. I mean, the times appointed for the solemn feasts of worship before the Living God.

They studied the movements of the stars and planets and understood chronological time. Remember God's comments about the beauty and purpose of the created lights. He said, diverse lights were made to tell signs and seasons, which bore physical and spiritual implications.

So, the Children of Issachar were responsible for calling the whole nation together when the stars aligned. Understand that the Jewish feast days were approximately based upon the lunar calendar, with consideration also given to the movement of the sun.

Also, bear in mind that, the people in that age could not access calendar as easily as we can today. As a result, the children of Issachar were able to call the nation to the mountain (Deuteronomy 33:19) to meet with God at divinely appointed times. What a task!

A Star in the Sky!

Wise men still seek Him...

Another group of people who displayed a level of discernment were the shepherds who identified a star in the sky.

This event is recorded in Matthew chapter 2.

Matthew 2:1-12 – New International Version

[1] "After Jesus was born in Bethlehem in Judea, during the time of King Herod, Magi from the east came to Jerusalem [2] and asked, "Where is the one who has been born king of the Jews? We saw his star when it rose and have come to worship him."

[3] When King Herod heard this he was disturbed, and all Jerusalem with him. [4] When he had called together all the

people's chief priests and teachers of the law, he asked them where the Messiah was to be born. ⁵ "In Bethlehem in Judea," they replied, "for this is what the prophet has written:

⁶ "But you, Bethlehem, in the land of Judah, are by no means least among the rulers of Judah; for out of you will come a ruler who will shepherd my people Israel."

⁷ Then Herod called the Magi secretly and found out from them the exact time the star had appeared. ⁸ He sent them to Bethlehem and said, "Go and search carefully for the child. As soon as you find him, report to me, so that I too may go and worship him."

⁹ After they had heard the king, they went on their way, and the star they had seen when it rose went ahead of them until it stopped over the place where the child was. ¹⁰ When they saw the star, they were overjoyed. ¹¹ On coming to the house, they saw the child with his mother Mary, and they bowed down and worshiped him. Then they opened their treasures and presented him with gifts of gold, frankincense and myrrh. ¹² And having been warned in a dream not to go back to Herod, they returned to their country by another route."

According to the above bible verses, the identification of the star in the sky by the shepherds was great, but their intelligence to follow divine instruction was more commendable.

We must be sensitive to know where and when to share sensitive information, and who to share it with.

King Herod's words were, "Go and search carefully for the child. As soon as you find him, report to me, so that I too may go and worship him."

But the reality is that he had no intention to worship the new-born child but to kill him.

The approach by the shepherds is another instance of discernment because if these shepherds had no divine interaction before they met the king, they would have disclosed strategic information because of the position of influence, of the person requesting it.

Divine intelligence will guide you in identifying who to disclose information with and when to or not to do so.

Many potent dreams, visions, and ideas have been terminated early because of the lack of discernment in disclosing information.

We must understand that because people inquire about your idea does not mean they are interested in its success.

Divine intelligence will guide your interaction, involvement and interests when dealing with people, irrespective of their position.

We see a similar story in 1 Kings 13:11-25 where an old prophet who had lost his relevance tricked a young prophet to his death because of a lack of discernment from the young prophet.

The intelligence referred to in this book will enable you to identify lies even from places where it is difficult to decipher a lie.

Take a look at verses 15 -19 of 1 Kings 13, the New International Version;

> ¹⁵ "So the prophet said to him, "Come home with me and eat."
>
> ¹⁶ The man of God said, "I cannot turn back and go with you, nor can I eat bread or drink water with you in this place. ¹⁷ I have been told by the word of the Lord: 'You must not eat bread or drink water there or return by the way you came.'"
>
> ¹⁸ The old prophet answered, "I too am a prophet, as you are. And an angel said to me by the word of the Lord: 'Bring him back with you to your house so that he may eat bread and drink water.'" (But he was lying to him.) ¹⁹ So the man of God returned with him and ate and drank in his house."

THE WOMAN WITH THE ALABASTER BOX
MARK14: 3-9

It was a time to relax for Jesus and everyone present. They were all in the house of Simon, the leper. Emphasis on 'the leper' is very symbolic!

In those days, people strictly avoided contact with diagnosed lepers to avoid the spread of this terrible and contagious condition to others.

Therefore, lepers were outcast of the land, and sent away to live alone. So, to eat at a Lepers house was not acceptable according to the Jewish tradition, except the individual has checked in with the priest to prove they were completely healed and entirely cleansed of all leprosy symptoms.

So, the fact that people ate at the house of 'Simon the leper' was a testimony to his healing by Jesus, the all-powerful healer.

Also, remember that Bethany was the village where Lazarus was raised from the grave after four days in the tomb. [Find this out in John 12:1-8].

Lazarus was present at the dinner party.

The unthinkable happened....
While Jesus was still reclining alongside the people present, suddenly, a woman walks into the room filled with Pharisees.

The woman's presence in the room already posed questions because it was culturally unacceptable and disrespectful for a woman to appear in such gatherings with majority of men present. And this woman seemed popular, because almost everyone in the room could identify her easily. Perhaps the way she dressed gave her away, or the people in the room had encountered her in some way known to them because Simon, in whose home this gathering was happening described her as a prostitute. The book of Luke chapter 7:37 describes her as 'the woman of the city'.

She went straight to Jesus, washed His feet with her tears, dried them with her hair, kissed the feet tenderly *and* caressingly and poured a very expensive oil on them, and this act raised attention and questions in the minds of the people present, especially Simon, the host.

This woman's outward appearance and what she was doing were identical with the description of the adulterous woman in the book of Proverbs 7: 10-18. Remember that the woman who had perfumes and dressed like a harlot.

Also, consider the disciples, who would not allow the master to touch their feet. How could they bear the sight of a harlot touching their master? Of course, they had difficulty accepting and appropriately interpreting what was going on.

But the reaction from Jesus was illustrative of the fact that the woman was divinely inspired. She was operating with supreme intelligence despite her disposition.

Surprisingly, not one religious person in the room, including the disciples of Jesus understood the significance of this woman's action. The woman had accessed divine revelation. She was operating from a dimension that religion could not access. The woman had bought into the schedule of heaven to prepare Jesus for His death, burial and resurrection.

Let us consider Matthew's account of the story;

Matthew 26:6-13 - New International Version

⁶ "While Jesus was in Bethany in the home of Simon the Leper,
⁷ a woman came to him with an alabaster jar of very

Unlocking Supreme Intelligence

> expensive perfume, which she poured on his head as he was reclining at the table.
>
> 8 When the disciples saw this, they were indignant. "Why this waste?" they asked. 9 "This perfume could have been sold at a high price and the money given to the poor."
>
> 10 Aware of this, Jesus said to them, "Why are you bothering this woman? She has done a beautiful thing to me. 11 The poor you will always have with you,[a] but you will not always have me. 12 When she poured this perfume on my body, she did it to prepare me for burial. 13 Truly I tell you, wherever this gospel is preached throughout the world, what she has done will also be told, in memory of her."

As expected, everyone there condemned her action, even though she worshipped Jesus. They all had an idea about what was wrong with everything that she did. However, Jesus knew that all she did was perfect and strategic for His burial.

Luke 7:37-38 – New International version

37 "A woman in that town who lived a sinful life learned that Jesus was eating at the Pharisee's house, so she came there with an alabaster jar of perfume. 38 As she stood behind him at his feet weeping, she began to wet his feet with her tears. Then she wiped them with her hair, kissed them and poured perfume on them."

Lessons from the story........

Everyone thought that her offering of the Alabaster box was a waste. But Jesus commended her for accuracy in understanding the timing of her offering.

Popular opinion is not always correct. Even though Peter and John were present, their actions proved they were not discerning.

Even in circumstances or events in our lives that don't appeal to human senses, God has a plan.

Unlocking Supreme Intelligence

Walk in supreme intelligence, and you will always be a step ahead of everyone, everywhere! Halleluyah!

Flesh and blood has not revealed this to you....

Matthew 16:13-18 - New King James Version

13 "When Jesus came into the region of Caesarea Philippi, He asked His disciples, saying, "Who do men say that I, the Son of Man, am?"

14 So they said, "Some say John the Baptist, some Elijah, and others Jeremiah or one of the prophets."

15 He said to them, "But who do you say that I am?"

16 Simon Peter answered and said, "You are the Christ, the Son of the living God."

17 Jesus answered and said to him, "Blessed are you, Simon Bar-Jonah, **for flesh and blood has not revealed this to you, but My Father who is in heaven.** 18 And I also say to you that you are Peter, and on this rock I will build My church, and the gates of Hades shall not prevail against it."

The bible verses above highlight the fact that there is certain information that cannot be accessed cognitively or intellectually but only divinely.

Communication and relationship with God give us access to what the natural man cannot access.

So, our problem most times is that we try to make sense of spiritual information or instruction when we should just comply and obey them.

The seeming foolishness of some spiritual instructions has deprived many of monumental victories and breakthroughs.

> *"Isn't it obvious that God deliberately chose men and women that the culture overlooks and exploits and abuses, chose these "nobodies" to expose the hollow pretensions of the 'somebodies'".*

Unlocking Supreme Intelligence

> **1 Corinthians 1:26-31 - J.B. Phillips New Testament**
>
> ²⁶⁻³¹ "For look at your own calling as Christians, my brothers. You don't see among you many of the wise (according to this world's judgment) nor many of the ruling class, nor many from the noblest families. But God has chosen what the world calls foolish to shame the wise; he has chosen what the world calls weak to shame the strong. He has chosen things of little strength and small repute, yes and even things which have no real existence to explode the pretensions of the things that are—that no man may boast in the presence of God. Yet from this same God you have received your standing in Jesus Christ, and he has become for us the true wisdom, a matter, in practice, of being made righteous and holy, in fact, of being redeemed. And this makes us see the truth of scripture: 'He who glories, let him glory in the Lord.'"

In Matthew 26, we saw how Jesus emphasized supreme intelligence.

Every other person gave a response based on what people said, 'some say'. But Peter bypassed what people thought or said and connected himself to a different dimension, a higher intelligence, *"You are the Christ, the Son of the living God."*

Operating with supreme intelligence will always make you stand out from the crowd.

It will bring peculiarity to your life.

Unlocking Supreme Intelligence

CHAPTER 4
The Kiss and The Sword

> *"Faithful are the wounds of a friend [who corrects out of love and concern],*
> *But the kisses of an enemy are deceitful [because they serve his hidden agenda]."*
> — **Proverbs 27:7 – Amplified Bible**

Sometimes, things are not usually the way they seem. Some situations and occurrences are more than ordinary observable phenomena. All through the Bible, there are several instances of people whose actions have had more implications than what they ordinarily did, and we will look at some of these people subsequently.

The woman with the box of alabaster perfume
(Matthew 26:7-13);

The woman in this story came to Jesus and anointed Him with costly perfume. Ordinarily, what she did seemed like a waste of resources because the speculation of the disciples was that they could have sold the perfume and the dividend distributed to the poor as it was worth two years wages.

Using a costly product on Jesus seemed almost contradictory to what Jesus represented as He modelled humility and moderation. However, the emphasis from Jesus was not on the literal cost of the oil but the significance of the woman's action. Jesus described the woman's action as *'beautiful'*.

Matthew 26:10 - New International Version

[10] "Aware of this, Jesus said to them, "Why are you bothering this woman? She has done a beautiful thing to me."

The Kiss and The Sword

Luke 24:1-6 - New International Version

¹ "On the first day of the week, very early in the morning, the women took the spices they had prepared and went to the tomb. ² They found the stone rolled away from the tomb, ³ but when they entered, they did not find the body of the Lord Jesus. ⁴ While they were wondering about this, suddenly two men in clothes that gleamed like lightning stood beside them. ⁵ In their fright the women bowed down with their faces to the ground, but the men said to them, "Why do you look for the living among the dead? ⁶ He is not here; he has risen! Remember how he told you, while he was still with you in Galilee:"

When others questioned the woman's action, Jesus Christ looked beyond that and considered the motive behind her action.

By her access to supreme intelligence, she had anointed Jesus at a specific time before His burial. The importance of TIMING!

Unlocking Supreme Intelligence

Access to supreme intelligence can prompt you to act outside human timing and plug into God's divine agenda.

Jesus' description of the woman's action is illustrated in Matthew 26:10;

> 10 But Jesus, aware of this, said to them, "Why do you trouble the woman? **For she has done a beautiful thing to me**"

Phillip the Evangelist

> **Acts 8:26-40 - New King James Version**
>
> 26 "Now an angel of the Lord said to Philip, "Rise and go toward the south to the road that goes down from Jerusalem to Gaza." This is a desert place. 27 And he rose and went. And there was an Ethiopian, a eunuch, a court official of Candace, queen of the Ethiopians, who was in charge of all her treasure. He had come to Jerusalem to worship 28 and was returning, seated in his chariot, and he was reading the

The Kiss and The Sword

prophet Isaiah. ²⁹ And the Spirit said to Philip, "Go over and join this chariot." ³⁰ So Philip ran to him and heard him reading Isaiah the prophet and asked, "Do you understand what you are reading?" ³¹ And he said, "How can I, unless someone guides me?" And he invited Philip to come up and sit with him. ³² Now the passage of the Scripture that he was reading was this:

"Like a sheep he was led to the slaughter
and like a lamb before its shearer is silent,
so he opens not his mouth.
³³ In his humiliation justice was denied him.
Who can describe his generation?
For his life is taken away from the earth."

³⁴ And the eunuch said to Philip, "About whom, I ask you, does the prophet say this, about himself or about someone else?" ³⁵ Then Philip opened his mouth, and beginning with this Scripture, he told him the good news about Jesus. ³⁶ And as they were going along the road they came to some water, and the eunuch said, "See, here is water! What prevents me from being baptized?" ³⁸ And he commanded the chariot to stop, and they both went down into the water, Philip and the eunuch, and he baptized him. ³⁹ And when they came up out of the water, the Spirit of the Lord carried Philip away, and

> the eunuch saw him no more, and went on his way rejoicing. [40] But Philip found himself at Azotus, and as he passed through, he preached the gospel to all the towns until he came to Caesarea."

By supreme intelligence, Phillip interrupted the journey of a very powerful man and led him to his salvation. An interruption and conversation that ordinarily could have been misread became a strategic moment in the saving of a government official.

Identifying and obeying divine intelligence is a necessity, and this can be instrumental in saving an individual, organisation and even a nation.

Phillip would have missed the opportunity to share God's word with the government official, had he tried to assess the opportunity logically.

The story of Phillip and the Eunuch emphasises that some opportunities are covered in risk, challenge and perhaps difficulty, but can be simplified and handled with divine intelligence.

Avoid the Kiss

It is better to be beaten by a friend than to be hugged by an enemy. In our lives, we must be careful of those who claim to love and care for us, as they might not always be who they try to portray themselves to be.be.

Judas was the treasurer in Jesus' ministry. As one of the executives, he claimed to love Jesus. However, he seemed to love money more, as he sold his master off with a kiss in exchange for 30 pieces of silver (Luke 22:47-48).

A kiss is supposed to be an intimate expression of love, affection and intimacy, but Judas used it as a mark of betrayal to identify Jesus during his arrest.

Another example is when Samuel was tasked with the mission to anoint the next king from the house of Jesse. He saw Eliab, the first born and immediately concluded that he was the man for the job because of his looks and appearance.

By implication, Samuel, a premier prophet, could have anointed the wrong person as king because of their physical appearance.

Unlocking Supreme Intelligence

Hence, in our lives, not everyone that appears right for us may be the right one. It takes alignment with God to discern whether the person we thought was God's choice is really God's choice.

We can gather from this story that God's choice on any matter can easily be misunderstood if considered through the lenses of our senses. Because something appears appealing does not mean that it is God. Because a person looks the part, sounds correctly, dresses nicely and talks fluently does not mean God is involved.

Our discernment must be very sharp. We must operate with supreme intelligence to fully align with God's will for our lives.

1 Samuel 16:1-13 - English Standard Version

[1] "The Lord said to Samuel, "How long will you grieve over Saul, since I have rejected him from being king over Israel? Fill your horn with oil, and go. I will send you to Jesse the Bethlehemite, for I have provided for myself a king among his

The Kiss and The Sword

sons." ² And Samuel said, "How can I go? If Saul hears it, he will kill me." And the Lord said, "Take a heifer with you and say, 'I have come to sacrifice to the Lord.' ³ And invite Jesse to the sacrifice, and I will show you what you shall do. And you shall anoint for me him whom I declare to you." ⁴ Samuel did what the Lord commanded and came to Bethlehem. The elders of the city came to meet him trembling and said, "Do you come peaceably?" ⁵ And he said, "Peaceably; I have come to sacrifice to the Lord. Consecrate yourselves, and come with me to the sacrifice." And he consecrated Jesse and his sons and invited them to the sacrifice.

⁶ When they came, he looked on Eliab and thought, "Surely the Lord's anointed is before him." ⁷ But the Lord said to Samuel, "Do not look on his appearance or on the height of his stature, because I have rejected him. For the Lord sees not as man sees: man looks on the outward appearance, but the Lord looks on the heart." ⁸ Then Jesse called Abinadab and made him pass before Samuel. And he said, "Neither has the Lord chosen this one." ⁹ Then Jesse made Shammah pass by. And he said, "Neither has the Lord chosen this one." ¹⁰ And Jesse made seven of his sons pass before Samuel. And Samuel said to Jesse, "The Lord has not chosen these." ¹¹ Then Samuel said to Jesse, "Are all your sons here?" And he said, "There

> remains yet the youngest, but behold, he is keeping the sheep." And Samuel said to Jesse, "Send and get him, for we will not sit down till he comes here." [12] And he sent and brought him in. Now he was ruddy and had beautiful eyes and was handsome. And the Lord said, "Arise, anoint him, for this is he." [13] Then Samuel took the horn of oil and anointed him in the midst of his brothers. And the Spirit of the Lord rushed upon David from that day forward. And Samuel rose up and went to Ramah."

Another instance was that of Paul, the apostle and the lady with a familiar spirit.

The evil spirit in the lady tried to deceive Paul by praising him. But Paul, being led by the Holy Spirit, saw the deceit and understood that she was only doing that to prevent the work of God from being accomplished. He then cast out the demon from her.

In our lives, there are instances where people or individuals try to deceive us into trusting them for their personal gains. We have to be very careful of these kisses, physical presentations or propositions, as they could do nothing but destroy our lives and stand as hindrances to God using us for His purpose.

> **Acts 16:16-18 - English Standard Version**
>
> ¹⁶ "As we were going to the place of prayer, we were met by a slave girl who had a spirit of divination and brought her owners much gain by fortune-telling. ¹⁷ She followed Paul and us, crying out, "These men are servants of the Most High God, who proclaim to you the way of salvation." ¹⁸ And this she kept doing for many days. Paul, having become greatly annoyed, turned and said to the spirit, "I command you in the name of Jesus Christ to come out of her." And it came out that very hour."

Embrace the Sword.

Be sensitive to the challenge strategic to your crown.

Sometimes, the best places for us to develop in life are the places where we feel challenged, uncomfortable or restrained. It is in the furnace of life that the precious stones of our lives emerge, shining and dazzling.

The three Hebrew boys, Shadrach, Meshach and Abednego are good examples of this thought. They were threatened with death because they would not bow down to the image of the King but stood their ground and later emerged from a fiery furnace alive.

By embracing the sword, which in their case was gruesome death in a fiery furnace, they entered their destinies and became rulers in a land they were originally taken to serve as slaves.

The **PROBLEM** Shadrach, Meshach and Abednego encountered ended in **PROMOTION**!

Daniel 3:19-30 - New International Version

[19] "Then Nebuchadnezzar was furious with Shadrach, Meshach and Abednego, and his attitude toward them changed. He ordered the furnace heated seven times hotter than usual [20]

and commanded some of the strongest soldiers in his army to tie up Shadrach, Meshach and Abednego and throw them into the blazing furnace. [21] So these men, wearing their robes, trousers, turbans and other clothes, were bound and thrown into the blazing furnace. [22] The king's command was so urgent and the furnace so hot that the flames of the fire killed the soldiers who took up Shadrach, Meshach and Abednego, [23] and these three men, firmly tied, fell into the blazing furnace.

[24] Then King Nebuchadnezzar leaped to his feet in amazement and asked his advisers, "Weren't there three men that we tied up and threw into the fire?"

They replied, "Certainly, Your Majesty."

[25] He said, "Look! I see four men walking around in the fire, unbound and unharmed, and the fourth looks like a son of the gods."

[26] Nebuchadnezzar then approached the opening of the blazing furnace and shouted, "Shadrach, Meshach and Abednego, servants of the Most High God, come out! Come here!"

So Shadrach, Meshach and Abednego came out of the fire, [27] and the satraps, prefects, governors and royal advisers

> crowded around them. They saw that the fire had not harmed their bodies, nor was a hair of their heads singed; their robes were not scorched, and there was no smell of fire on them.
>
> ²⁸ Then Nebuchadnezzar said, "Praise be to the God of Shadrach, Meshach and Abednego, who has sent his angel and rescued his servants! They trusted in him and defied the king's command and were willing to give up their lives rather than serve or worship any god except their own God. ²⁹ Therefore I decree that the people of any nation or language who say anything against the God of Shadrach, Meshach and Abednego be cut into pieces and their houses be turned into piles of rubble, for no other god can save in this way."
>
> ³⁰ Then the king promoted Shadrach, Meshach and Abednego in the province of Babylon."

Another important example in scripture was Daniel, who was thrown into the den of lions but came our unscathed. Daniel 6:16-28

God went before him to make the lions his friends. He eventually emerged as a conqueror and became one of the most important and influential people in Babylon. By

The Kiss and The Sword

embracing his sword, he was promoted, and his life never remained the same.

At some point in life, for us to make progress, we will come face-to-face with challenges, but if we persevere, become tenacious and never give up, we will surely emerge victorious.

GOD BLESS YOU!!!

Unlocking Supreme Intelligence

PART B

How to Gather Spiritual Intelligence

Unlocking Supreme Intelligence

CHAPTER 5
Learning The Art of Spiritual Mapping

> ³ "A house is built by wisdom and becomes
> strong through good sense.
> ⁴ Through knowledge its rooms are filled with
> all sorts of precious riches and valuables."
> — *Proverbs 24:3-4 – New Living Translation*

The art of Spiritual mapping helps us to see things beyond the physical; it can be compared to the use of X-rays, MRI (Magnetic resonance imaging) or CT (Computerised tomography), used to create detailed images of the inside of the body, with the aim to understand and diagnose what can be seen on the outside of the patient.

Strangely, not everyone understands that the invisible world is as real as the physical environment; some think that it is only a myth, but the truth is that the spiritual is in control of the physical world. So, there is great need to be aware of this truth.

In other to better understand the Art of spiritual mapping, let's delve a little into the concept of Remote sensing:

Remote Sensing

Remote sensing is a general term for computerised geographical data collection at a distance from the subject area. It is simply a method of collecting data on a particular location without having physical contact with that location.

An example is a satellite image capturing the image of the earth's surface. Just as in the natural, we have topography, which is the study and description of the physical features of an area. The spirit of God is bringing our consciousness to the spiritual representation of topography.

The prophet Elisha prayed for the eyes of his servant to be opened in order to identify the resources available to them that could not be identified with the physical eyes.

> 17 "And Elisha prayed, "Open his eyes, Lord, so that he may see." Then the Lord opened the servant's eyes, and he looked and saw the hills full of horses and chariots of fire all around Elisha."
>
> **- 2 Kings 6:17, New International Version**

But these horses and chariots of fire could not be physically identified.

These resources were available to both Elisha and his servant in the same location, but the servant could not see it.

Divine intelligence will give you access to what is available to you that nobody else can see.

Unlocking Supreme Intelligence

Identifying your available resources through divine intelligence brings peace, in the face of an overwhelming opposition.

2 Kings 6:8-17 - New International Version

8 "Now the king of Aram was at war with Israel. After conferring with his officers, he said, "I will set up my camp in such and such a place."

9 The man of God sent word to the king of Israel: "Beware of passing that place, because the Arameans are going down there." 10 So the king of Israel checked on the place indicated by the man of God. Time and again Elisha warned the king, so that he was on his guard in such places.

11 This enraged the king of Aram. He summoned his officers and demanded of them, "Tell me! Which of us is on the side of the king of Israel?"

12 "None of us, my lord the king," said one of his officers, "but Elisha, the prophet who is in Israel, tells the king of Israel the very words you speak in your bedroom."

Learning The Art of Spiritual Mapping

> ¹³ "Go, find out where he is," the king ordered, "so I can send men and capture him." The report came back: "He is in Dothan." ¹⁴ Then he sent horses and chariots and a strong force there. They went by night and surrounded the city.
>
> ¹⁵ When the servant of the man of God got up and went out early the next morning, an army with horses and chariots had surrounded the city. "Oh no, my lord! What shall we do?" the servant asked.
>
> ¹⁶ "Don't be afraid," the prophet answered. "Those who are with us are more than those who are with them."
>
> ¹⁷ And Elisha prayed, "Open his eyes, Lord, so that he may see." Then the Lord opened the servant's eyes, and he looked and saw the hills full of horses and chariots of fire all around Elisha."

In the natural, we have surveyors who help determine accurately the terrestrial or three-dimensional space position of points and the distances and angles between them using levelling instruments such as theodolites, dumpy levels and clinometers.

Hope for you too

It is also given unto you to know the mystery and secrets that pertain to your life, family, ministry, business, community, nation etc.

My emphasis on all of this is to highlight the importance of

DISCERNMENT, which gives you the ability to do the following:

- Hear intelligently, by attention and obedience
- Separate mentally, distinguish or understand
- And to know or ascertain by seeing

Hear intelligently, by attention and obedience!

There is a need to go beyond listening, but to hear and listen intelligently to divine instructions each time the Lord speaks. It is giving all your attention to the voice of the Lord and obeying promptly. Just think of the consequences that happened to Moses after hitting the rock three times when the instruction was only to hit it once. The failure to obey completely marked the end of his life. How about Saul? Learn from the lives of these men and ensure you hear intelligently by giving your entire attention to God's word, with the powerful ability to make you wise.

To separate mentally, distinguish or understand.

It is essential to understand the things of the Spirit. Hearing intelligently will be of no value if the receiver cannot interpret or understand the spiritual message received. The Chief Butler and the Chief Baker both had dreams they could neither understand nor interpret.

Thank God for men like Joseph who could interpret their dreams for them.

Now, picture how disastrous it would have been for Egypt if there was no one to interpret Pharaoh's dream.

Through divine intelligence, Joseph, while interpreting Pharoah's dream, gave Pharoah a business strategy that saved and stabilised the economy of the nation during famine.

Applying this principle of hearing intelligently and interpreting spiritual messages correctly to life, an inability to operate with divine intelligence can have devastating consequences.

> **Genesis 41:34-36 - English Standard Version**
>
> [34] "Let Pharaoh proceed to appoint overseers over the land and take one-fifth of the produce of the land of Egypt during the seven plentiful years.
>
> [35] And let them gather all the food of these good years that are coming and store up grain under the authority of Pharaoh for food in the cities, and let them keep it.
>
> [36] That food shall be a reserve for the land against the seven years of famine that are to occur in the land of Egypt, so that the land may not perish through the famine."

And to know or ascertain by seeing

The term 'seeing' in this context does not relate to the physical sight. We look but not with the physical eyes.

Ecclesiastes 2:14 - Amplified Bible, Classic Edition

14 "The wise man's eyes are in his head, but the fool walks in darkness; and yet I perceived that [in the end] one event happens to them both."

The wise man, because of his ability to see beyond his present circumstances, can plan for the future; hence, he's not overtaken by misfortune, and even when challenges appear, he has the wisdom to navigate through them. The wise don't pray for storms to stop. They don't pray for challenges to go away. They don't pray for problems to stop. On the contrary, they pray for the wisdom to solve them.

2 Corinthians 4:18 - Amplified Bible

18 "So we look not at the things which are seen, but at the things which are unseen; for the things which are visible are temporal [just brief and fleeting], but the things which are invisible are everlasting and imperishable."

This is what the apostle Paul in writing to the Ephesians, described as *'the eyes of your understanding being enlightened'*.

Ephesians 1:18 - New King James Version

18: **the eyes of your understanding being enlightened**; that you may know what is the hope of His calling, what are the riches of the glory of His inheritance in the saints,"

Ephesians 1:17-19 - The Message

15-19 "That's why, when I heard of the solid trust you have in the Master Jesus and your outpouring of love to all the followers of Jesus, I couldn't stop thanking God for you—every time I prayed, I'd think of you and give thanks. But I do more than thank. I ask—ask the God of our Master, Jesus Christ, the God of glory—**to make you intelligent and discerning** in knowing him personally, your eyes focused and clear, so that you can see exactly what it is he is calling you to do, grasp the immensity of this glorious way of life he has for his followers, oh, the utter extravagance of his work in us who trust him—endless energy, boundless strength!"

Prayer Points:

- *Ask God to give you light in your mind.*
- *Pray that God would give you divine intelligence.*
- *Pray and ask God for the wisdom to navigate through any kind of challenge you may encounter.*

James 1:5-6 - New King James Version

5 "If any of you lacks wisdom, let him ask of God, who gives to all liberally and without reproach, and it will be given to him.

6 But let him ask in faith, with no doubting, for he who doubts is like a wave of the sea driven and tossed by the wind."

Behold, a Troop is coming!

There is a generation rising that will be able to spiritually sense and discern things from a distance and collect and release data by the influence of God's spirit.

They will have insight into other countries and nations through the influence of God's spirit, People who will discern things without physically being present.

CHAPTER 6
How to Secure the Anointing for *Discernment*

---

²⁻⁴ "Consider it a sheer gift, friends, when tests and challenges come at you from all sides. You know that under pressure, your faith-life is forced into the open and shows its true colours. So don't try to get out of anything prematurely. Let it do its work so you become mature and well-developed, not deficient in any way.

⁵⁻⁸ If you don't know what you're doing, pray to the Father. He loves to help. You'll get his help, and won't be condescended to when you ask for it. Ask boldly, believingly, without a second thought. People who "worry their prayers" are like

> wind-whipped waves. Don't think you're going to get anything from the Master that way, adrift at sea, keeping all your options open."
>
> **- James 1:4-8 - The Message**

In the previous chapters, we noticed the importance of discernment in the life of every Christian because, by it, we are enlightened. Discernment also helps to bring insight into matters hidden from the natural man.

As we have earlier considered, the sons of Issachar were knowledgeable people who did not just follow the crowd in their resolutions and behaviour but acted on the wisdom of God in every situation of life. They were sensitive to subscribing to God's leading rather than popular opinion.

Let us consider certain things we must do, to operate like the sons of Issachar in the subsequent discussions:

1. Ask..... *'Let him ask'*

> **James 1:5 - English Standard Version**
>
> ⁵ "If any of you lacks wisdom, let him ask God, who gives generously to all without reproach, and it will be given him."

The Bible says in Matthew 7:7 *that we should ask, and we shall receive.* If we carefully seek God and diligently ask him for the anointing of the sons of Issachar, he will surely answer our prayers and give heed to our pleas. If we ask God for the ability to discern, He will surely answer us in His mercies, and nothing good will be withheld from us. All of God's promises are available to us. All we must do is ask Him in the place of prayer.

2. Expect

> **James 1:6-8 - New International Version**
>
> ⁶ "But when you ask, you must believe and not doubt, because the one who doubts is like a wave of the sea, blown and tossed by the wind.
>
> ⁷ That person should not expect to receive anything from the Lord.
>
> ⁸ Such a person is double-minded and unstable in all they do."

When you have asked God for a thing in the place of prayer, expect to receive it, even when it seems like all you have asked for is not coming to actualization. When it seems to you as though your prayers are not being answered, do not feel bad, maintain your prayer posture, bringing God to the remembrance of His words and promises.

For example, in Babylon, when everything seemed so difficult, it looked like the Israelites would never leave the land of slavery. Daniel prays to God. He acknowledges that God upholds his promises to those who obey his commands. For those of us unfamiliar with covenants, these were essentially two-party agreements. If you upheld your end of the deal, the other party was required to do so. Often, if you broke a covenant, it resulted in death. It is with this understanding that Daniel approached God in prayer.

When the anointing is now on you...

The anointing or influence of God upon a person is not limited to the altar, but it is very much needed in every aspect of our life, as we have seen in chapter three of this book. To reiterate, we must leverage God's anointing for exploits because it is the anointing that makes the difference.

Therefore, when the grace and anointing of God are at work on an individual, it becomes noticeable to people who encounter them. That is because the anointing empowers you to do things that ordinarily seem impossible with your physical strength and abilities.

For the individual, a shift happens within you, and you begin to notice the presence of that uncommon ability and enablement to undertake things that would naturally overwhelm you, projects that would frighten you in the past.

The divine influence on your life becomes that guiding force that motivates you to act upon a conceived idea or even refrain from something. Just like the children of Issachar, that supernatural influence will cause you to function with divine timing and a boldness that cannot be shut down by any human force.

My prayer for you is that reading this book will position and align your heart in readiness to receive and function with divine intelligence.

CHAPTER 7
How to Respond to Divine Intelligence

> *"Discretion will watch over you, Understanding and discernment will guard you".*
> — ***Proverbs 2:11 – Amplified Bible***

Our level of spiritual sensitivity must be very high regarding the promises of God in our lives. We, therefore, must be alert to discern spiritual activities around us and consequently shield our promises from people with evil intentions.

It is important to understand that your good intention will not necessarily be perceived as good or acceptable by everyone around you.

Our response to any spiritual signal coming to us must be with promptness.

Don't be naive, not everyone can be trusted with everything. There are people whose plan is to take everything and everyone down by one simple move.

Therefore, discretion is of high importance!

The unique message of this chapter is centred on how to respond to supreme intelligence.

The absence or lack of spiritual intelligence can cause destruction

In Hosea 4:6, God was speaking when he said, "my people are destroyed because of the lack of knowledge".

To replace the word *'destroyed'*, some other versions used words like,

Perish, doomed, cut-off, silent, ruined.

How to Respond to Divine Intelligence

God didn't say the people are destroyed because they don't have a promise on their life, but rather because they don't know.

Also, knowledge in this verse was not related to human knowledge, rather it emphasised ignorance. There was the absence of *recognition and revelation* of God's word. Their spiritual senses were dull, and the ones to guide them, priests and prophets were also dull.

The people could read the word but lacked revelatory knowledge to guide them in acting on the word.

If you carefully read Hosea 4:6, you will discover that the problem in that text, was due to the lack of RECOGNITION of REVELATION.

The problem was a lack of spiritual intelligence. The ability to get insight beyond the letter. The ability to see the spirit beyond the letter. The life-giving aspect of the word. (2 Corinthians 3:6)

> A lack of REVELATION can leave you in TRIBULATION.

> An absence of REVELATION can leave you in AFFLICTION
>
> A lack of REVELATION can leave you in OPPRESSION
>
> A lack of KNOWLEDGE can bring you HEARTACHE

The verse in Hosea 4 highlighted the danger of living without divine revelation.

It also shows that a people or nation can be under bondage and suffer severe poverty, not because they are not blessed, but because they don't recognise they are blessed.

Not because there's no promise on their lives but because they are unaware or lack the spiritual insight to recognise the blessing.

So, because of ignorance or lack of spiritual sensitivity, people are walking away, migrating and leaving a place that God designed and programmed to bless them.

By divine intelligence an individual can live and prosper in a land deemed worthless.

How to Respond to Divine Intelligence

By divine intelligence, a nation can deploy and win a war with strategies that are considered foolishness.

We see this in the battle of Jericho.

> **Joshua 6:1-5 - New International Version**
>
> ¹ "Now the gates of Jericho were securely barred because of the Israelites. No one went out and no one came in.
>
> ² Then the Lord said to Joshua, "See, I have delivered Jericho into your hands, along with its king and its fighting men.
>
> ³ March around the city once with all the armed men. Do this for six days.
>
> ⁴ Have seven priests carry trumpets of rams' horns in front of the ark. On the seventh day, march around the city seven times, with the priests blowing the trumpets.
>
> ⁵ When you hear them sound a long blast on the trumpets, have the whole army give a loud shout; then the wall of the city will collapse and the army will go up, everyone straight in."

In verse 2 of Joshua 6, the promise of God was established and clear, "See, I have delivered Jericho into your hands, along with its king and its fighting men."

But the tactics to claim what had already been promised were unfamiliar to Joshua and his men. It required some level of spiritual intelligence.

Be quick to act on divine intelligence.

When you get a word from God, one delayed move to act swiftly on that word can be detrimental to you and others. When God gives you divine intelligence, be sensitive and swift to act.

If you take a look at our global political climate, most of what has caused devastating effects on individuals, cities and even nations resulted from people who took too much time to deliberate on military intelligence. Instead of acting swiftly on intelligence, they delayed in taking action.

A delayed response to divine intelligence can be detrimental.

The point is, although the threats were indeed identified, and on many occasions, the people or forces behind it were

How to Respond to Divine Intelligence

located, too much time was taken to deliberate on the corresponding action to dismantle or control the situation.

It will interest you to know that while we take considerable amount of time to over-analyse this intelligence, the enemy is still on schedule to carry out their plans. When the enemy discovers their location and operations have been compromised, they accelerate their plans to execute earlier than the initially projected timescale to destabilise their opponents.

The importance of acting immediately on divine intelligence was seen in the story about the prophet Elijah in 1 Kings 17.

The brook dried up, and God scheduled a supply operation for the prophet, but this supply was time sensitive because he had to go immediately.

⁹ "Go at once to Zarephath in the region of Sidon and stay there. I have directed a widow there to supply you with food."
(1 Kings 17:9 - NIV)

He arrived at the city gate and interestingly, by divine intelligence identified his supply, a widow gathering sticks.

His supply was disguised as an insignificant widow. We read later to discover that his supply also needed a supply, the woman was in need too. But God's intelligence never misses.

However, this is where most people miss it. We arrive at the place based on God's divine intelligence to discover that it physically contradicts our expectations.

But we must learn to trust God.

1 Kings 17:7-11 - New International Version

[7] "Sometime later the brook dried up because there had been no rain in the land.

[8] Then the word of the Lord came to him:

[9] "Go at once to Zarephath in the region of Sidon and stay there. I have directed a widow there to supply you with food."

> ¹⁰ So he went to Zarephath. When he came to the town gate, a widow was there gathering sticks. He called to her and asked, "Would you bring me a little water in a jar so I may have a drink?"
>
> ¹¹ As she was going to get it, he called, "And bring me, please, a piece of bread."

Be sensitive, people are tied to your divine intelligence.

The gift of supreme intelligence is not meant only for personal use, but God has put it in us to also affect other lives. There are people in your sphere of influence you are equipped to impact, but others can't.

The Bible has a long list of great men and women who stepped out in faith by applying divine intelligence, and we could see that just a singular act affected even the unborn generations to come.

The bible verse we read earlier in 1 Kings 17 sheds light on this.

Though the prophet Elijah was in need, his provision was linked to the supply for the widow.

It means that if he had not immediately acted on divine intelligence, the widow and her family would have been affected.

Sentiments often cause people to ignore warnings picked up by discernment and spiritual sensitivity, and this can have devastating effects on people, destinies, families, marriages and ministries. It can shut down churches and businesses. It can destabilise the political and economic structure of a nation.

Many are in captivity not because the enemy is powerful but because they ignored divine intelligence, due to emotion and sentiments.

Like King Saul in 1 Samuel 15, they would make sacrifices instead of making strategic decisions and obeying God.

Now that we are aware of this, we must be responsible to function with divine intelligence, understanding the benefits when we respond quickly and the potential consequences if ignored.

> **1 Samuel 15:22-23 - New Living Translation**
>
> ²² "But Samuel replied, "What is more pleasing to the Lord: your burnt offerings and sacrifices or your obedience to his voice? Listen! Obedience is better than sacrifice, and submission is better than offering the fat of rams. ²³ Rebellion is as sinful as witchcraft and stubbornness as bad as worshiping idols. So, because you have rejected the command of the Lord, he has rejected you as king."

Delayed obedience is disobedience in itself.

Say these Prayers with faith as you set your heart to respond to divine intelligence.

1. *Heavenly Father, I pray that as I come to a point in my life where I dare to ask You to reveal Your will for me, You would put me in a place of acceptance of what You reveal to me. It may not be what I want,*

but it will surely be what I need to live a life fully invested in you. ***(Romans 8:26-29, 2 Corinthians 12:5-9)***

2. *Heavenly Father, help me to realize that anything you bring into my life and anything you reveal to me is for my good. Give me a spirit of acceptance and a heart open to your movement in my life.*

3. *Allow me to let your love surround me and cast out any fear or doubts. Help me to live in love with you, accept your will for my life and give me the proper response to your revelation. May I trust in the way you push me to go.*

4. *Father, give me a heart like that of Mary's, willing to agree with Your Word, Your promises, and Your intent for my life. With Mary, there was no negotiating, no hemming or hawing, no 24 hours to think about it, and no keeping her options open. You simply spoke, and she unhesitatingly responded with a 'Yes'.*

   You have an intent for me. That purpose will have its challenges, its high points and low points, but

> *Your plan is far and above the best plan for my life.* ***(Luke 1:38)***

5. *May my soul be transformed into one that instantly obeys You, comes when You call, follows Your lead, and believes Your Word even when I can't fully comprehend it, for Your Word is Truth. In Jesus' Name, Amen.*

6. *Father, I ask that as you begin to provide me with divine intelligence, that my spirit is sensitive to understand and act swiftly without fear or favour, and without sentiments. That your intentions will be executed on earth as it is in heaven.* ***(Matthew 6:10)***

I believe, in this season, God is raising a generation of people who will step out by faith and act on the moment.

People like Peter who said, Lord, if it is you, ask me to come. (Matthew 14:22-33)

You should hear this very loud and clear.

Some People who will see God's word as a foundation will step out and build, irrespective of what the topography report of that area represents.

People who see God's word as a foundation will invest in the unlikeliest of places and businesses because God directed them.

These people will stand for politically elected offices against the popular opinion and win.

People who will defy sentimental connections and do what God has placed in their heart, not what they feel like doing, but what God by His Spirit has stirred up in their hearts.

I hear this; *I will put a desire in their hearts,* desire to do my will, things they have not previously imagined.

This is God's word for you. All you need to do is step out in faith.

GOD BLESS YOU!!!

For more information on teachings and outreaches,
or to book Dabo Davies, please visit
www.dhdavies.org
or write to
info@dhdavies.org

Printed in Great Britain
by Amazon